THOUGHTS
for the
GRIEVING CHRISTIAN

by Doug Manning

In-Sight Books

1st printing–February 2001

Copyright© 2001 by In-Sight Books, Inc.
P. O. Box 42467
Oklahoma City, Oklahoma 73123
1-800-658-9262
www.insightbooks.com

Manufactured in the United States of America

ISBN 1-892785-38-2

Cover Photo by Ted West Photography

In Memory of Katie Schwartz

Contents

Introduction v

Section I If Faith is the Victory, Is My Pain a Defeat?
Jesus Wept 11
David Ate 16
Faith Has Two Edges 22
Job's Friends Still Live 28
Doing Unto Others 34
Why? 40
Blame 47
The Gift of Choice 53

Section II The Grieving Process
The God of the Process 61
As Unique as a Fingerprint 67
Grief's Dark Valley 72
Now About that Cussing 79
Will it Ever Get Better? 85

Section III Expectations
Christianity is Addition Not Subtraction 93
Lonely In a Crowd 97
Fear Even in Faith 102
Something Happened to My Want To's 106

Section IV Gifts for the Journey
The Gift of a Message 113
The Gift of an Ear 118
The Gift of Community 123
The Gift of Presence 129
The Gift of Hope 135

Bibliography 140

Introduction
He Spoke in Parables

I have always marveled at the way Jesus taught his disciples. Long before psychology was even thought of, or the theories of teaching were born, He knew how learning happens. He told parables or stories. We have heard these stories for so long and so often that we cannot relate to how difficult it was for the disciples to grasp and understand what He was saying. These were stories with complicated meanings and were hard to understand. They had not heard anything like this before, and the stories left them struggling for insight.

Jesus would tell one of these stories and then just walk away, leaving the group scratching their heads in wonder. "What did he mean by that?" was the most common response. If, at a later time, the disciples wanted to know what He meant they were expected to ask. If they asked He would patiently explain, but He only explained after they had spent time scratching their heads in wonder.

Real learning and growth demands those times of scratching heads in wonder. The most valuable time of His teaching ministry was that period between the telling of a story and the explanation, while they were struggling for light within themselves.

This book tries to follow that same model. I hope to make statements that create thinking and stir up feeling on your part. There will be pauses and a place for your thoughts following each statement or story. We might add a short thought, a poem or a scripture to aid in your thinking process, but the most valuable part of this book will be those things you discover. If you write them, they become more deeply a part of your experience and can be referred to again and again. I am certainly not Jesus, but together we can apply His great teaching principle to your pain.

—*Doug Manning*

v

Section I

If Faith is the Victory, Is My Pain a Defeat?

Write down the thoughts of the moment. Those that come unsought for are commonly the most valuable.
–Francis Bacon

Jesus Wept

One of the things people found most remarkable and, to some, the most despicable about Jesus was his friendship with women. Responding to a woman as an equal was unheard of in that day. It also made Him many more enemies than friends. He did not hold mass rallies for women's rights, He just led by example and openly loved and respected each one He met. Two such friends were Mary and Martha. He seemed to find great peace in their presence and in their home.

Their brother, Lazarus, became ill and Jesus did not arrive until after he had died. The sisters were in deep grief and anger over his death, and even expressed some of that anger toward Jesus. "If you had come in time our brother would not be dead" is a heavy load to place on a friend. Jesus did not express any anger at this outburst. He seemed to accept anger as a normal response to grief. His response to Mary and Martha pictures God's acceptance of our anger in times of sorrow. Even our anger at Him. They were angry, and He loved them anyway.

Then He did a most unusual thing. He sat down and cried. That would not be unusual if He were not Jesus, but that was who He was. That would not be unusual if He did not know that He was going to resurrect Lazarus in a very few moments, but that was what He was going to do. In spite of all of that, *Jesus wept* (John 11:35 KJV).

We all know that He wept. The shortest verse in the Bible is "Jesus wept." We learned that so we would have a bible verse to quote when asked by some Sunday School teacher. We use this verse as a means of pulling a joke on the teacher, but in our jesting we miss the poignancy of those two words. The fact that there are only two words adds to the power of the moment. There is no need for any further explanation. He cried. What else would you expect Him to do? Even though He knew all about Heaven, even though He was going to raise Lazarus from the dead, this did not save even the Son of God from a broken heart.

No matter how close He was to a resurrection,
it still hurt to lose a friend.

If that was true of Jesus it must be even more so for us. We do not know what He knew. We know of Heaven only as a future experience we hope is true. We cannot perform resurrections, and have never seen one. Maybe what those short two words means is:

No matter how close to God we are,
loved ones still die

No matter how much faith we have,
we will still grieve.

No matter how much Heaven means,
it is still lonely now.

No matter how close we are to the
resurrection, it still hurts when a
loved one dies.

Sorrows are our best educators.
A person can see further through a tear
than a telescope.
—Lord Byron

David Ate

King David's son was dying. He prayed and fasted until the death came, then said something to the effect that he could not bring his son back, but he could go to him. Then he had supper. I cannot recount how many times I have heard that quoted as the way a Christian is to respond to the loss of a loved one. Too often we are made to think we are supposed to be above grieving. If we have faith, our grief will be limited to a brief period of time and then we are to get up and go about our lives as if nothing has happened. I recognize that is how David did it, but I do not know how he became such a model for us in the area of fatherhood, or anything else. If the Scriptures say anything about David, they say he was a very flawed person whom God loved anyway. His response to his son's death may have more to do with denial than it does with faith.

If we are not careful, we will decide that real faith produces stoicism. The more stoical we are, the more we show our faith.

We also seem to think that stoicism is a sign of strength and good breeding. I wish Jackie Kennedy had cried at the funeral of her husband. We treasure the scene of her standing bravely while John John saluted his father. The whole country seemed to sigh and say, "What dignity, what grace, what strength in time of sorrow." Somehow that has crept into our society until showing pain is a sign of weakness and lack of faith.

Stoicism does great harm. An airplane crash took the life of a young business man. He left a wife, a son who was eleven and a daughter of nine. I became involved with this family years later when the daughter was tragically killed at age twenty-four. The daughter had experienced a long history of struggle in her life. As we explored the history we came face to face with the aftermath of a stoical approach to grieving. Since the crash happened before the time when we began to study grief, there was no source of help for the family. There were no books, no support groups, and their friends were just as much in the dark about grief as the family.

The mother heard the daughter crying in the night and went to her bed. The mother also was crying as she asked the daughter how she could help. The daughter said, "If you would just quit crying. It hurts me when you cry." That night they made a pact to stop crying. They shut down all expressions of their grieving together. Many of the problems the daughter had to face later in life, started that night. The mother made a profound effort trying to help her daughter get through the loss. She acted out of the only knowledge available at the time. The stoical stance they fought to retain from that night on took a toll on their lives.

When we try to control grief we are asking for trouble in the future. I think grief is one of the major social problems of our day. We do not see it as a social problem but we have no idea how many of the things we call social problems come from grief that is not properly dealt with and is allowed to fester until it expresses itself in some of the activities we call social problems. Substance abuse, eating disorders, and divorce are often the result of swallowed grief.

Stoicism takes great energy. Keeping our feelings under control takes almost all of the energy we have. In time we run out of strength and must find some way of relief. Too often the relief comes in alcohol or drugs. We can't be in control and drunk at the same time, so it is a release. We can't be held responsible for our actions if we are drunk or drugged at the time, so we can let ourselves go and blame it on the chemicals or the alcohol. Far too many people have had to use some substance to fill in for the lack of expressing their grief.

Stoicism traps the family. I am not the only one who is hurt if I choose to be stoical about my grief. Everyone else must also be stoical when I am around. It silences the whole family. Those who want to talk are effectively hushed. Those who need desperately to grieve are handled. It locks the entire family group in a prison of silence. We dare not cry. We dare not talk. We dare not show our grief. Prisons never heal.

David may have gotten up and gone on, but the Scriptures are full of other folks who howled long and loud when they were in grief. The prophets cried out to God in pain. Moses argued long and loud about many things. Job said he wished he had never been born. Jesus stood at the tomb of a friend and wept. Stoicism is not faith, it may just be fear.

Suffering in silence is highly overrated.

Tearless grief bleeds inwardly.
–C. N. Bovee

Faith Has Two Edges

A person who did not like me very much once asked me if all good preachers were smart alecks. The question meant I was either not a good preacher or I was a smart aleck. Maybe I was both. I answered that all the ones I had known were. The same thing that lets a person be free enough to get in front of people and take a chance on being a fool, tends to make them be somewhat overbearing when they aren't in the pulpit. When I married, someone gave me a book that said, "Every fault has a virtue on the other end of it and every virtue, when carried to the end, has a fault." Everything in life has two sides. Every sword cuts two ways. That thought has helped me become more accepting of others and of myself.

Even something as wonderful as your faith has two edges. On the one hand it will heal. On the other hand it can cause pain.

Your faith will be a sustaining force as you walk grief's journey. It will mean you are not alone. There will be times when you cannot feel His presence. There will be times when you wonder if He is even alive. When you feel the weakest and the most alone, there will be something deep inside that lets you know He is there.

You may be full of doubts and fears.
You may be angry about what has happened
to your loved one.
You may feel weak and undone.

Even in those times there is something inside that clings to faith. I look back on my life and must say there has never been a time when I didn't know He was there. There have been times when I was ashamed of being who and where I was. There have been times when I wished He did not know where I was or what I was doing. Even then, I knew. That is faith.

That faith will help you cling to hope when there is no reason to hope. It will help you fight to find meaning when there seems to be no meaning to be found.

The same faith that sustains you in your journey can also be a source of struggle. You can become guilty because your faith is not as strong as you expected it to be. Often we have lived rather sheltered lives with little or no pain to face. We have gone to church, sung the songs and heard the messages of God's wonderful love and how the true heroes of the faith have stood up to life's tests. It was easy to tell ourselves that we, too, would stand. Nothing could ever make us doubt our God nor shake our faith. Then the world collapses and suddenly it isn't as easy as we expected. There is no way to know the devastation of loss and grief until you are faced with it in your own life. Then, and only then, do you really know what these experiences do to a faith. It is easy to begin pressuring yourself because you don't feel as strong as you thought you would. Or you don't feel as close to God as you think you should.

If having faith means you cannot be weak or angry, or have doubts about the very existence of God, then you will be faced with a load of guilt too heavy to bear. You are going to have some of these feelings. Their presence does not mean you do not have faith. Nor do they mean you have done something to cause God's presence to leave. All these things mean is that you are a human being suffering the things human beings suffer and reacting to the pain.

Faith can become a burden if it is used as pressure to perform. Most of your friends will not be comfortable with your grief. They want you to get well because they care about you, of course, but they also need you to get well for their own comfort. It is far too easy to use faith as a means of pressuring you to at least act well even if you aren't.

They may fill the air with platitudes about the faith. Or hint that you are not believing as you should. One friend of mine lost her husband shortly before Christmas. Her pastor's wife said, "I know this is a hard time for you, but aren't you glad to know that John is spending this Christmas with Jesus?" She answered, "Not at all, he should be spending it with me." I like her answer. She was not going to allow anyone to use the faith as a pressure point for her behavior.

"Faith talk" may even cause pain and anger. If a plane crashes, those whose loved ones died are crushed to hear the survivors tell wonderful stories about how God was with them and saved them from the disaster. Those who lost loved ones are left asking why God did not do the same for their loved one.

Your faith is much too important to allow it to become a source of guilt or struggle. Right now it may not be very strong. Right now God may feel distant and unreal. One thing is for sure. We serve a God who lost a son and knows what those losses do to the comfortable belief system we thought would never be shaken.

The Reverend John Claypool's daughter suffered from leukemia. She had been in remission and they thought she was going to make it. Then she relapsed and headed toward her ultimate death. During that ordeal, John preached a sermon on Isaiah 40 that says, *"We shall run and not be weary, we shall walk and not faint."* His message was, "I am barely walking. I cannot run and not be weary. All I can do is barely walk, but that is all right with both God and me." If you can't run, then walk without guilt.

Hope is hearing the melody of the future;
faith is dancing to it today.

—Ruben A Alvez

Job's Friends Still Live

Most of the help you will receive in your grief journey will come from your friends. Unfortunately, a great deal of the hurt will also come from your friends. They mean well. They sincerely want you to be better. Most do not know what to say. Many will be scared of the intimacy involved and want to change the subject as quickly as possible. Some will avoid you altogether. In the middle of all of this pain, you will find one or two people who have been there and know what to say and do. They will be angels sent from Heaven itself.

Job had three friends who came to give comfort. His pain was so great all they could do at first was tear their own clothes, throw dust on their heads and sit in silence for about a week. That doesn't sound like much help, but when life caves in nothing feels better than the presence of a friend. They were a great source of comfort to Job, as long as they were silent. They listened as he lamented. They did not flinch when he wondered about the existence of God. I call that "laying ears on folks," and it is healing.

Then they spoke. They couldn't take it any more. They had to give Job the benefit of their vast wisdom. I have noticed a pattern in how people talk to the grieving. Since the pattern is so ingrained it must be instinctive.

First we explain. There seems to be an overwhelming urge to explain why things happen. Most of the explanations you will hear are designed to defend God more than comfort you, but the explanations will come. With the very best of intentions someone will say something like was said to one of my friends. His little girl was killed in a car wreck and a person said, "Perhaps your little girl would have grown up to be a bad person, and God took her home before that could happen." Somehow in this person's mind that was supposed to be comforting to this devastated father.

We explain because we think we can change the way you feel by changing the way you think. Feelings don't always follow thoughts. There will be times when you will think your pain would go away if someone would just tell you why this happened. There are no explanations that can adequately answer your questions, and, if there were, they would not make the pain go away. I don't think a change of thinking takes away pain.

If explanations don't work, people will begin to argue. You will hear all kinds of lectures that begin with, "Now you can't let yourself feel like that," or, "Now you know…" Friends want you to be better so deeply that they will begin forcing it upon you, if necessary. They do not understand that grief is a journey, a long journey, and it must be walked through an inch at a time. They want to push you through to victory.

If explanations fail, even close friends will criticize. You will begin to hear, "You are not trying to get well." "You are wallowing in your grief." "It is time to put the past behind you and get on with your life." Sometimes the criticism is subtle. Sometimes it is blunt and harsh. It is never a comfort.

I felt so smart when I discovered that pattern. Then I reread the book of Job and found out the friends of Job were following that pattern in the oldest book in the Bible, long before I came along. The three friends were named Eliphaz, Bildad, and Zophar. Eliphaz spoke first and he explained the workings of God in great detail. He based his explanations on his personal experiences with God and on insight he thought came directly from the throne room.

Bildad was the one to argue, "There is no way this kind of thing could happen to you unless there was a reason. You must have done something wrong."

Zophar was the critic. He told Job that he deserved more than he got.

There will be those who must explain, those who must argue, and even those who must criticize the way you face your grief. Fortunately there will be those who "stick closer than a brother" and give strength when you have none of your own. You can find a support system of safe people.

Maybe there are some points to ponder:

God does not gossip. He does not talk about you to others. No matter how convincing they sound, they do not know the will of God for you.

In grief you need people who will simply be there, hug you, and hush. Look for the sound of silence.

You need some "safe" people and a "safe" place for your grief. It might help to make a list of those who can give the most help. Think through what help you want from them and then be bold enough to tell them how they can be one of your "safe" people.

Why can't somebody give us a list
of things everybody thinks and nobody
says, and another list
of things that everybody says
and nobody thinks?
—Oliver Wendall Holmes

Doing Unto Others

One of the baffling aspects you face in your grief journey will be what to say to your friends. On the one hand you want to relate as a Christian person. On the other hand you probably don't know what to say. One of the statements I hear the most often is, "How am I suppose to respond when people ask me how I am doing?" When people ask, you probably don't know whether they really want to know or just don't know anything else to say. You may want to say, "How do you think I am doing?" But that would not be nice, so you say *fine* even though that is not true, and both you and the person who asked knows it isn't. That response gets them off of the hook, but it leaves you cold and lonely.

You will find yourself growing tired of trying to figure out how to respond. I have heard many people say that if they had to answer the "How are you" question one more time they just might explode.

Sometimes people will not just inquire about how you feel, sometimes they will say things that hurt. Often they will have no idea they have just stabbed you in the heart and will blithely go on with the conversation while you stand there bleeding unnoticed.

Often the things they say will add to the pressure you already feel. When they say, "Don't you find great comfort in knowing your loved one is better off?" you may want to scream, "NOT AT ALL," but inside you wonder why don't you feel like that. Is there something wrong with you or your faith?

The Struggle for Friends

Unfortunately, grief brings a struggle for friendship along with the pain. Some friends will fail you. Some of the ones you just knew you could count on no matter what you had to face, will be strangely absent. They cannot figure out what to say, and the strain of not knowing is more than they can face. They are not comfortable around feelings they cannot control so they avoid. Some will even get angry with you and justify the anger by saying you are not trying to get well.

Some will want to help and will try to be with you at every possible moment, but somehow you will not be comfortable in their presence. They may be old friends, but suddenly there does not seem to be anything to talk about when they are there. It seems to be a strain and you don't know why. They don't say anything wrong, but you don't feel as if you can bare your soul to them. You feel awkward and are relieved when they leave. Then you feel guilty because of your feelings.

Some will come across as far too sure about life's answers. Even the spiritual things you once thrilled to hear can create discomfort right now. That does not mean these things are not so. It does not mean you will never enjoy talking about them again. It only means there is a time and a place for all things. When you are in the throes of pain and doubt, too much certainty can confuse instead of bless. Right now you want someone to cry with you. Almost everything else will not help.

Principles

You are the only expert in your grief. You are the only one who knows how you feel. You are the only one who knows what makes sense during this time of pain. You are the only one who knows what is confusing instead of comforting. You alone know what you need.

You must be free to seek that which helps. If going to prayer meetings at every possible chance is what you need right now, then that is where you should be. If avoiding such meetings for a time is what helps you, then that, too, must be your choice. This is not the time for fitting into other people's plans for your healing. You will know what works and what helps. Do those things without guilt.

You will find comfort in strange places. I have been amazed at some of the things people have found to be of great comfort. Thoughts that sound almost silly to me have been expressed with such fervor and joy that all I could do was stand amazed. Activities I never would have thought about have proven to be a source of great relief to some individuals. You will find that which hits you in the right places. No matter what the thought or action may be, if it helps it is healthy.

You alone can educate your friends. You can tell them what you need and what works. There will be certain friends that you will want to educate. The more honesty you can bring to this process the more freedom you will discover.

You must be free, however, to chose whom you wish to educate. It takes a certain kind of person to give comfort. The ones who help you may not be your closest friends. The choice must be yours. No one else knows.

You also must be free to decide when you don't want to be bothered with educating friends. Sometimes you will not have the emotional energy to even try. Sometimes you just won't care whether you ever try or not. There are times when it will just be easier to say, "I am fine" and walk on by.

You must be free to speak. It is appropriate to say, "I don't see it that way." It is not being rude to say, "That is not how I feel right now, I may come to that place in the future, but right now that does not fit me." You must have the right to defend your own emotions without fear. Your true friends will stay with you. They may be shocked and flustered in the process, but if they really love you, they will stick it out. The ones who don't stick, aren't really friends. Try to avoid getting caught in situations that force you to fake being better than you are. "Fake it till you make it" is too great a burden to carry.

Survival is not selfish. We are built by God with a basic instinct to survive. If someone yells FIRE our first instinct is to get out of the building. We may later think of others, but at that moment we want to be safe. When grief stalks our world the instinct to survive is stronger than any other. God made us this way, and He did so for good reason. He loves us and wants us to survive the pain. To do so, our own feelings must take top priority. This is the time to heal you. The rest will come later, first you must be nurtured back to health. That is priority one.

I was sitting, torn by grief.
Someone came and talked to me of God's
dealings of why it happened, of why my loved
one had died, of hope beyond the grave.
He talked constantly. He said things I knew
were true. I was unmoved, except to wish he'd
go away. He finally did.

Another came and sat beside me.
He didn't talk. He didn't ask me leading
questions. He just sat beside me for an hour
and more, listening when I said something,
answered briefly, prayed simply, left. I was
moved. I was comforted.
I hated to see him go.

–Joe Bayly

Why?

A minister may have said it best. We were at a grief support meeting for families who had suffered the death of a child when he said, "I have always believed and taught that we could pray to the Father for protection and He would send His angels to watch over us. Then my daughter was killed by a drunk driver. From that night on, I have not known what to believe."

Many of us were raised believing that Christians were somehow immune to tragedy. Other folks died young. Other people divorced. Other people suffered great losses in their lives, but Christians—that is, "good Christians"—were not subjected to these things.

Of course, all the time we were believing this, Christians were dying, divorcing and suffering all around us. We were able to either close our minds and not see the reality of this, or we worked it out to be some kind of exception to the rule. Maybe these folks were not as close to God as they seemed to be. Perhaps this was punishment for some sin in their lives. Or maybe God allowed this to happen to teach them some lesson or make them better Christians. We would struggle for a little while and then dismiss the whole issue with "It must be God's will and all things work together for good."

Some folks find it easiest to just blame all bad things on the Devil. I heard a minister on television say, "Christians are not victims of circumstance. Everything that happens to us is either from God or the Devil." That is an easy answer until we begin to ask how the Devil got so much power in our lives. Usually the answer makes it our fault.

No matter what theology you were raised on, now that a great loss has hit your life, nothing seems to be an adequate answer and nothing seems to be able to explain the "why" in the middle of your heart.

Why did this happen?
Why did this happen to me?

All of the reasons and explanations sound like hollow clichés and meaningless platitudes. All of your reasoning ends up facing a blank wall of pain.

To make matters worse, you may not be at all sure that you have the right to ask the questions. Who am I to question God? Statements like "Ours is not to reason why, ours is but to do or die" begin to flood your minds with condemnation and fear.

I stood dumbfounded while a lady said, "The Lord giveth and the Lord taketh away, blessed be the name of the Lord," to a friend of mine who had just been told her daughter had to have a dangerous operation. Does that mean we are to accept without question and even be glad no matter what we must face?

Do you have the right to question? Do you have the right to complain? Do you have the right to be angry? Do you have the right to grieve? Are all of these basic emotions denied to you by a loving God? When you decided to follow Him, did you become less equipped to face the pains in life? Is God more interested in your being tough and true than He is in your getting well? It is more than evident that bad things happen to Christians. What is not evident is how Christians are suppose to react to these bad things.

One of the greatest sermons I ever read was delivered by John Claypool after his thirteen-year-old daughter died. The sermon was called "Life Is Gift." In the sermon John tells of a letter he received from a minister named Carlyle Marney. Dr. Marney said, "John, God's got a lot to give an account for." At first John was shocked and repulsed by the statement. It sounded like blasphemy. The longer he thought the more he realized that God does have a great deal to give an account for. The wonderful thing about our faith is that God will give such an account. He will not treat us like a leaf that falls from the tree with no reason given. There will come a day when the God of the universe will sit with His children and explain in great detail the story of our lives. It boggles the mind to think about, but everything about a God so great, and yet so loving, boggles my mind. Faith is not belief without question. Faith is believing there are answers and being willing to wait until God's time to understand the why's.

Believe me, the first time there is question and answer session in Heaven, I am going to be on the front row with my hand up. I have stood by too many graves after too many senseless deaths. I have held too many hands and searched the heavens for words of comfort that did not help after the death of a child. I have walked through too many valleys of my own not to have questions, and, though it is more than I can dare believe, I have the right to ask all of them.

There Are No Good Answers

There really aren't any good answers to why we suffer. I don't know why bad things happen to good people. One of my favorite stories is about a young seminarian who went to sleep in class. The professor stopped teaching and stared at the young man until he suddenly awoke under the stare. The professor said, "Young man tell me why there is evil and suffering in the world." The student stammered out, "I...I used to know the answer to that question but I forgot." The professor turned to his class and said, "Mark this day well. In the history of the world there have only been two people who knew the answer to that question. One was Jesus and he did not tell us—the other was this young man, and he forgot."

Maybe the best answer I know is that if bad things only happened to bad people we would all be good for the wrong reasons. Unfortunately that sounds so inadequate when you are hurting.

One analogy that makes sense is that life is like a card game, and fate deals the cards. We want God to deal them and we want some way to insure He will give us nothing but good cards. In this analogy, He set it up so that life itself would deal. His role is to stand beside our chair and help us play whatever cards we draw. That helps some, but I still want Him to deal.

Answers Will Not Heal

All morning long a mother kept saying, "If someone will just tell me why! Why was my son killed in a car crash? Why did it happen to him? Why me? If someone will just tell me why! I think I can handle it, if someone will just tell me why." I did not argue with her nor try to explain until well after lunch. Then I asked if I could tell her what I was hearing her say. She gave permission and I said, "I keep hearing you ask why. There is nothing wrong with asking why. I would not take that right away from you in any way. You have the right to question. You have the right to question God Himself. You have the right to do more than question. You have the right to be angry with Him. But, behind your questions I am hearing you say that if you could just understand why this happened the pain would go away. Is that what you are saying?"

She said, "Yes, I guess I am saying that." I said, "I wish I could answer your question. I wish I knew the why's to our pain. But even if I did know, even if I had an answer so clear you could not deny a single point and even if it were presented with such clarity that you could believe it all the way to the inner most recesses of your being, the pain would still be there. You are not hurting because you don't have answers. You are hurting because your son has died. No answer will make that pain go away. No philosophy will make it all better. No theological explanation is going to change the way you feel."

This may sound rather hopeless to you. Most of us were raised in a cause and effect world. There was a logical reason for everything that happened to us. Life was simple. Everything was black and white. Now you stand in a world that does not make any sense at all, and I have just told you there really are no simple or logical answers to your basic question. The goal of your grief journey is not to find an answer. The goal is to learn how to cope with your loss and live again. If answers would do that, the Bible would be full of them. They are not there because your loving Father knows the path must be walked and that the help you need is His presence and the love of some of His folks. That is the source of the help you need. But, some kind of answer would sure be nice.

Mourning...is an undoing.
Every individual tie has to be untied and
something permanent and valuable
recovered and assimilated from
the knot...Blessed are they that mourn for
they shall be made strong, in fact.
But, the process is like all human births,
painful, long and dangerous.
                                    –Margery Allingham

Blame

Since I was raised in a black and white world of simple answers to every question, I was also raised in a world of God controlling and punishing His people. If I did something wrong I expected to suffer some kind of punishment. I was raised believing that if I did not tithe, God would cause all kinds of setbacks and suffering to happen in my life. One of my very favorite preacher friends used to say, "Everybody tithes. Some bring it in, God has to go collect the rest. But He gets His tenth one way or another." I could never understand how doctor bills or car repairs and tithing could be the same to God, but I loved my friend and believed his words.

This kind of thinking easily led to my being afraid that, if I did wrong, God would punish me through my children's suffering. If they became ill, I froze in fear. Is this when the punishment starts?

Early in my ministry, I was inundated with families in pain. Children died. Cars wrecked. Murders happened. Cancer took lives. All of these tragedies happened to wonderful people. People who were strong in their faith.

I could no longer ignore the real world, and I could not find answers to the questions the real world forced me to face. Did God take that couple's baby to punish them? Did He let it happen to teach them some lesson they could not learn any other way? Did He do it to deepen their faith?

A minister friend of mine had a car wreck that killed his little girl, and almost took the lives of he and his wife. I sat up in the hospital most of that first night waiting to see what the outcome would be and trying to comfort the family. Another pastor was also present. After several hours the pastor said, "Doug, the church where I pastor and the church pastored by the man in the wreck were having an attendance contest. Do you suppose God was displeased with our contest and caused this to happen because of that displeasure?"

That was the world I was raised in and that kind of thinking still rears up in our souls when a tragedy comes. Did God cause this to happen because of something I did?

This kind of thinking may be keeping you awake and in a cold sweat late into the night.

My fears forced me to dig into the Scriptures trying to understand how God deals with His people. I started in Genesis and worked my way through the entire Bible studying the concept of punishment. The study began with increasing fear and foreboding. I read such things as "…visiting the iniquity of the fathers upon the children, and upon the children's children, unto the third and to the fourth generation" (Exodus 34:7 KJV). Maybe God did take the life of my friend's little girl because of an attendance contest.

But the Bible is a developing revelation. It started where the people were and gave them as much light as they could receive then. As they developed, the revelation developed. What they were hearing in Genesis is not what they were hearing as they grew nearer and nearer to the absolute revelation in Jesus. As I followed the trail of enlightenment, I found a growing concept of a God of love.

Most people love Psalm 23, and quote it for comfort. I also love that poem, but as strange as it may seem, my favorite verses in the Old Testament are found in Ezekiel 18. When I found these words, I wept for joy.

> These are the words of the Lord to me:
>
> What do you all mean by repeating this proverb in the land of Israel: "The fathers have eaten sour grapes and the children's teeth are set on edge"?
>
> As I live, says the Lord God, this proverb shall never again be used in Israel. Every living soul belongs to me; father and son alike are mine…"
>
> —Ezekiel 18:1-4 NEB

That means God does not use one life to affect another life for either blessings or punishment. God does not parlay one life against another. He does not use someone else to impact your life.

If your loss causes you to grow, fine, but
that is not why this happened.
If growing through your loss deepens your faith, that is
wonderful, but this is not some act of God designed
for that purpose.

We live in an imperfect world. We live in a world that has cancer, car wrecks and violence. We live in a world where children are born with no hope of life. We live in a world of so much despair that some wonderful people cannot find a way to go on. In that world a certain number of people will have cancer. A certain number will have a car wreck or some other calamity. Within that number there will be a certain percentage of Christians. That percentage will not be any smaller or any larger than normal statistics would predict.

God has never promised us that we would be immune from the normal percentages of life. As the old song said, "I beg your pardon, I never promised you a rose garden." Our hope is not in finding some way to get God to never let anything happen to us. Our hope is not in finding some easy answers when things happen anyway. Our hope is finding the resources He has for us to help us face whatever cards life deals.

Most of the time, the finding of those resources starts when the fear and guilt stop. I do not know what you are struggling with as we talk, but I do know you did not cause this to happen.

The secret of my success is that at an early
age I discovered that I was not God.
—Oliver Wendell Holmes, Jr.

The Gift of Choice

There is a legend of a sculptor who formed a statue of a beautiful woman and placed it in a park. Every day, without fail, the sculptor would visit the statue. He loved looking at the form and beauty of the woman. Over time he fell in love with the woman in the statue. He would quote poems to her, have long talks about how she filled up his lonely life, and pour out his love to her with warmth and passion.

One night an angel appeared to the sculptor in a dream and asked if he wanted the woman in the statue to become real. The sculptor said, "I would rather have that than anything in the world. If she becomes real, we can love each other and be together always." The angel reminded the sculptor that if she became real she could also choose to not love him. She might walk with him for a while and then find someone she loved more. She might even reject him from the start.

The sculptor said, "Leave her there. I would rather her be there and be all mine than to take a chance on losing her." In reality, the sculptor did not love the woman in the statue, he loved himself and what the woman could do for him.

No analogy is perfect, but God had a similar choice when He created us. He had to decide whether to make us so we had to love and follow Him, or give us freedom and hope we did so. He could have made us into robots or puppets that He could control without question. He could have clutched us to Himself and used us to fulfill some need or niche in His world.

Had that been His choice we would never have known any struggles or problems. We would never have felt the sting of guilt or the responsibility of wrong choices or behaviors. We would also never have known the joy of love, for love can only be love when it is freely given. We would never have known the joy of growth, for growth comes from personal choices and struggles. We would never have known the joy of creativity or thinking, for these can only happen in an atmosphere of freedom.

Life would have been a peaceful hell of repetition and meaningless-ness. All of the wonders of this world come from His choice to make us free. Free to love Him, and free to reject Him. Free to follow His path, and free to follow the temptations of other plans. He wanted us to enjoy life, more than He wanted us to either behave or perform for Him, so we are free.

The freedom He lovingly gave and the freedom that gives us every-thing lovely in our lives, also exposes us to the pains and tragedies of life.

Choice means the possibility of bad choices.
Choice means we become responsible.
Choice means some people are free to hurt us.
Choice means the world will never be at peace.
Choice means we will face pain and struggle.

Freedom means we will stand beside the grave of a
child and never understand why.
Freedom means we will walk through valleys too deep
to imagine and struggle with our own healing.
Freedom means God does not do nearly as much for
us as we wish He would.
Freedom also means that God had to pay an awful cost
to win our free will decision to
come follow Him.

I have spent my life walking neck deep in pain. A senseless murder of a friend by her own husband, suicides where I felt deep loss and numb-ing responsibility. Healthy children found dead in their beds with no cause ever discovered. A beautiful young woman killed with no remorse or reason. A grandson born on Christmas Eve and died on Christmas day with only thirty four hours of life.

I have spent my life being misunderstood by people I cared about. Lied about by people I helped. Stolen from by people I trusted.

And Yet...

I will never stop being grateful to God that He chose to set us free.

I will be eternally grateful for the right to face and struggle and weep and mourn and fight for my sanity caused by that one choice to set us free.

I am a person—not a robot—not a statue in the park—a person with all the good and bad that name brings. I am a person, thank God, I am a person.

If God did everything His power could do
or everything we asked Him to do
human life would shrivel into nothingness;
for it is in the struggles to survive
that we find life.

–Doug Manning

Section II

The Grieving Process

Immortal? I feel it and know it
Who doubt it of such as she?
But that is the pang's very secret
Immortal away from me...

Your logic, my friend, is perfect
Your moral most drearily true;
But, since the earth clashed on her coffin,
I keep hearing that, and not you.

Console if you will. I can bear it;
'Tis a well-meant alms of breath;
But not all the preaching since Adam
Has made Death other than Death...

Communion in spirit! Forgive me,
But I, who am earthly and weak
Would give all my incomes from dreamland
For a touch of her hand on my cheek...

–James Russell Lowell
After the Burial

The God of the Process

As Christians, it is easy for us to think that if God is at work the results must be instantaneous and miraculous. If I have a cancer that goes away after a single prayer meeting, that is of God. If my cancer gradually recedes after long and painful bouts with chemotherapy, that may be from God, but it is somehow not the same. We want our cures to come from some kind of instant zapping from God. Those kinds of cures make us feel more like God is at work.

Grief is God's way of healing a broken heart, but it is not instantaneous nor miraculous. It is a long term walk through our pain. There are no shortcuts. There are no miracle cures that take all the pain away. It is a step-by-step process toward learning to cope with a broken heart that will never heal. A portion of your heart has been taken away and it will not grow back. You will learn to live again, but the pain will always be there. Over time it will become a dull ache, but you will hurt and mourn the loss as long as you live. *And God is in the process.* Just because it is slow does not mean He is not at work.

I think He lets us walk through the process because that is the healthiest way for us to deal with a loss. Grief that is not faced does not go away. It sits there and festers until it exemplifies itself in some other way. It sounds like a great spiritual victory for someone to stand and announce how God has taken away their grief just a few short days after a death has occurred but, as a person who has studied grief for many years, such stories scare me. I have seen the results of unresolved grief and worry about what lies ahead for those who place themselves in that position.

There is a naturally progressive pattern to grieving. We are designed by God to walk through this process toward healing. Grief is not an enemy to be avoided. Grief is not a sign of weak faith to be shunned. Grief is a natural way to deal with the feelings as they surface. You are doing your best job with grief when you are grieving. It is when you are losing it that you are dealing with the feelings that have surfaced.

Grief comes in waves of various feelings. You have no control of the waves. There is no way for you to predict when a wave will come. They hit, you cry, or talk, or scream, or take a walk, or sit quietly and sob, until the wave passes and there is a little time of relief. When the wave is hitting and you are reacting, you are moving through the grieving process. When you hurt the worst, you are doing the best job with grief. That is tough and we wish there was some instant relief, but instant relief leaves all of those feelings locked inside to eat away at your soul.

When I speak with Christian groups, I can never explain this right, but since it is just the two of us maybe I can. I tell people they must keep their "cussing current". When I say this I am not advocating the use of foul language. I differentiate between cursing and cussing. Cursing is using foul language. Cussing is the expression of feelings. It is saying "I am mad," when you are mad. It is screaming in the night when nothing else seems to give relief. It is hitting a hammer against a nail with serious intent to do damage. Those are the feelings we need to release. That is why God created grief. It is His way of saying, "It is all right to be sad. It is all right to cry. It is all right to get angry. It is even all right to get mad at me."

This process lasts much longer than most people think. Your friends will give you about three months and then start hinting that you should be "getting on with your life." A quarterback ruptured his Achilles tendon. The commentator said the quarterback would be out of action for at least two years and no one had any argument with that time table. We have seen others suffer this kind of injury and we know it takes that long to heal and rehabilitate. No one thinks the guy is weak or not trying if he is not back in three months. Broken hearts, however, are suppose to mend quickly or we don't have much character or faith.

The grieving process takes a minimum of two years. Some will take much longer. That does not mean you are going to hurt the way you hurt now for two years. It just means that it takes that long for the feelings to surface and for us to work through enough of them so we can begin to live again. Giving yourself permission to take as long as you need to complete the process is the very best thing you can do for your own healing. The process goes so much better if you are not fighting yourself because you aren't progressing as fast as you think you should. That takes too much energy and you already know you are short in that department.

The title of my second book was *Don't Take My Grief Away From Me.* The basic message of the book was that our efforts should not be aimed at taking away our grief, but at facing it and dealing with the feelings involved. I still believe that to be the healthiest approach to grieving. I also believe that is why God does not intervene and make our pain go away. Healthy grieving only happens when we grieve.

What wound did ever heal but
by degrees.
–William Shakespeare

As Unique as a Fingerprint

There are no experts in grief. No one knows how your grief will progress nor what you will feel. Grief is as unique as a fingerprint. Each person's grief is unique to that person and to that grieving experience. I have talked with people who were having a hard time understanding why their second grieving experience was so different from the first. One woman reported that when her son died she reacted so violently that she had seizures. There were no seizures when her husband died, so she wondered if she did not love her husband as much as she did her son or if she was not grieving properly. Neither was true. We react to each loss in a way that is appropriate to that loss.

There are no set patterns that must be followed. Almost every author who writes about grief lists some stages of grief. I listed four stages in *Don't Take My Grief Away From Me*. However, I was having trouble with the "stages" idea even then. Stages sound too much like distinct lines of demarcation. They sound like grief is an organized movement through a predetermined pathway. In truth, we flip flop through the stages. I think we can be in two of them at the same time. There is no set pattern for when feelings will surface. There is no way to predetermine how you will react when the feelings do surface. There are some generalized periods to grief that seem to be fairly consistent in almost every grieving experience, but they cannot be put into any set order that fits everyone.

Who knows what questions you will have or when they will come to the surface?

Who can predict what feelings will overwhelm you or in what order those feelings will come?

As long as you are allowing the grieving process to happen, there is no right or wrong way. There is no time table. There is no being early or late in your journey. This is your journey and you will walk it in your way. I often say that we grieve like we do everything else in life. Some make fast decisions and move on. Others take more time in decision making and ponder the results longer and deeper. Your grieving will reflect those patterns that fit you.

In very general terms, there is a period that I call the whirl. When I described grief in stages, I called this the shock stage. In most cases there is a time when it is real and yet not real. You know it happened, but you expect to wake up at any moment and find it was all a dream. You cry and hurt, but it is like going to a sad movie. You expect the movie to end, the credits to roll, and you walk out into the bright lights again. Your mind will make an intense effort to let you face reality as gradually as possible. I call this a whirl because that is how most folks describe the experience. Your mind seems to be racing at a fantastic rate. There are thousands of questions whirling in your head, but you cannot focus on them long enough to ask and receive an answer. Reality is whirling there also, but it hits and runs. After my brother died, I would have a flash thought that I would never see him again. Before I could react to that reality the thought was gone and several others were flashing by. It was all a whirl.

There seems to be two tracks running through the whirl. One track says, "I cannot stand this pain. I will not survive. This is more than I can possibly endure. I am weak and fragile and it is hopeless." The other track wants to jerk God out of Heaven and say, "Why did You do this to me? Why did You let it happen? Did you know it was going to happen? Where are your angels?" We spend a great deal of time jumping from track to track—alternating between fear of survival and the urge to anger.

If you are in the whirl, the most important thing I can say is "Feel what you feel." Don't fight your feelings. There is no right or wrong way to grieve. You must be free to deal with the feelings you have when they surface and you must be free to do it your way.

*The only courage that matters is the kind
that gets you from one minute to the next.*
—Mignon McLaughlin

Grief's Dark Valley

At some point the whirl stops, and reality dawns. Cold and hard it comes to lead you into the dark valley of grief. You wake up in the night realizing you will never see your loved one again. This time it does not flash and go away, it settles on your chest until you can't breathe. Your chest hurts. It is amazing how much actual physical pain there is in grief. No one prepares you for the pain, and then it hits.

You call a friend and don't know what to say or why you called. You cry until there seem to be no tears left in your body but then they start again. Despair settles into your very being and you know there is no way you can survive. The Psalmist said, "Yea, though I walk through the valley of the shadow of death, I will fear no evil…" (Psalms 23:4 KJV), but you aren't the Psalmist and the valley seems deep and fearful.

This is the toughest part of your journey. There is no denial to soften the blow. There is no dream to wake from. There is only the harsh reality that the loss is real and your loved one will not suddenly be there again.

The waves come harder and seem much
heavier than before.

The load seems far beyond your ability to bear.

Your prayers may seem hollow and empty.

There is no way around the valley. It must be walked through. You cannot medicate the pain away. When the pill wears off the pain is waiting right where you left it.

You cannot drink the pain into numbness. Alcohol is a depressant and just makes the melancholy deepen into hopelessness.

I cannot make the pain go away. I cannot "put the best face on your loss" so it won't seem so bad. I cannot cheer you up by telling you how much worse it could have been or how much worse someone else's grief is. I cannot explain why God allowed this to happen and let that explanation somehow make sense. When you are walking in grief's dark valley, nothing makes sense.

I can tell you that you are on a journey and you will not always be in the valley. Grief is transition. Where you are today is not where you will be tomorrow. There will be a time when the waves are not as often or as heavy. There will come a time when you live again. That may be of some help, but probably not as much as both of us would like.

Right now the only thing that matters is how to get through today, this time, this valley. I have some suggestions that have helped others and I hope they prove to be what you need also.

Find safe places. Find a place where it is all right to grieve. Where it is all right to not be in control. Where no one is going to panic and try to stop the tears. Where you will not need to "keep it together because they will not understand." Survival is not the number one goal, it is the only goal. Nothing else matters—what friends may think, how friends may feel, whose needs you are not able to meet—none of these matter right now. There will be plenty of time to deal with all of these issues later. Friends will return and you can mend any fences that are down. There will be some place or places where you feel safe. That is where you need to be. Go there and do not feel any pressure to be anywhere else until the storm passes.

Find safe people. You may well find that the friends or family members you thought would be the best help are either not available or you are not comfortable with them. There may not be any logical explanation for this, but you just can't be with them for very long. Quite often the ones who help the most were, at best, distant friends before the loss, and yet when the chips are down, they are the ones you feel safe with. Sometimes the safest people will be those you meet in a grief group. You did not know them before the loss, but they feel like old, warm friends from the first meeting. Cling to those people.

Some will call and hint that their feelings are hurt because you do not have time to see them. Some may call for lunch and you want to say yes, but something inside won't let you go. The guilt can make the valley deeper. It is appropriate to say that right now you are just not up to lunch or too much company. Thank them for their interest and hang up your guilt at the same time you hang up the receiver.

Don't be afraid of losing it. I guess the most pressure you will feel will be the fear of breaking down in the wrong places. Trying to keep it together and keep the upper lip stiff is not easy and not healthy. That is why you should spend most of your time in safe places with safe people. Places and people you do not mind seeing you with a blotchy complexion, swollen eyes and a red nose. People who love you just the way you are. That is safety and safety is necessary when the valley is darkest.

Find ways to say it. Talk until you wear out several sets of ears. You must actually talk grief to death. When you are talking you are dealing with the feelings that surface. You may say the same thing over and over. You may think you are boring people to tears. It may seem that you are whining your life away. You may think you are wallowing in your grief and some may even say you are, but nothing takes the place of talking through the feelings.

Write. The main reason this book offers space for journaling is that writing out your thoughts, feelings and fears is a great way of dealing with your grief. You may not write well. You may have trouble concentrating long enough to make sense, but it will help to write out what you feel inside.

Have a good scream. I received a call late one night from a woman in Michigan. She said she had crumpled in the floor and could not get up. Her husband and son had died in a car crash and her grief had become so overwhelming that she crumpled to the floor. When I asked her what she felt like doing she said she felt like screaming. I urged her to do so and she screamed for several minutes. She must have felt foolish screaming into a phone to a person she had never met, but she let it out anyway. Suddenly, she stopped, said "Thank you, I feel much better," and hung up the phone. I never heard from her again.

Screaming is a great outlet for feelings. You may not feel free enough to do it in front of even your safe people, but it is healthy in private as well. Find a place and let it rip.

Find ways to show it. Everyone gets tired of telling people how much they hurt or how much they need a hug. I urge families to pick out a stuffed bear and make it the designated hugger bear. When you are in need, go find the bear and give it a hug. It feels good and it is a great way to signal to the rest of the family that you need some attention right now. They find out and you did not have to say anything. This works great with children. The best way to get a hug, is to let someone know you need one.

Hang on. That does not sound like much comfort, but the truth is you must just hang on through the valley. The day will come when you will find hope and joy and peace. Hang on until morning dawns in your valley.

*I have grown to believe that even as these
losses have broken me, so can they heal me...When
someone I love dies, I buy a candle. There are
twelve across my mantle now:
one for my father, one for my mother, one for my
daughter, two for my grandfathers, and seven for
my babies who were born too soon.
It is a simple, comforting act to light them in
reverent remembrance of each life. Whenever
anyone stops to count these candles, the question I
am most frequently asked is, "How did you do it?
How did you survive?" My usual answer:
"I don't know."*

–Dana Gensler
Twelve Candles
LARGO Newsletter

Now About that Cussing

I don't use that term just to shock people or to be controversial, although it does serve that purpose. I use it because I have a hard time explaining the presence of anger to people in grief. Most never recognize any anger at all. Some feel compelled to search for the signs of anger and don't think they are doing their grief right until they can find it. So I just say all of the feelings of frustration, hurt, disappointment, rejection and fear, all of them need cussing over. We need to express how we feel. We need to tell the world that we have been hurt. That is what I mean when I say cussing. As I have already explained, I am not talking about the use of dirty words. I am talking about the use of whatever words that express the feelings that are there.

You may never feel what you would identify as anger, but there is anger in grief. Anger is the natural response to hurt, and grief is a deep hurt so anger should be there. You may never be able to define it in those terms, nor really define what you are angry about, but the feelings of anger will be present. The anger is healthy. It is one of the motivators that drive you through your grieving process. The surfacing of these feelings rescues you from the depths of the valley. Basically you hit bottom and get mad. If we were talking about stages in grief this would be the reaction stage. This is when you begin to heal. It is also when your friends and family will think you are not doing well at all. You are no longer the fragile soul who cannot function. Suddenly you are the person who is telling the world how much you dislike what has happened to you.

Even though the anger is healthy, you still need to find ways to let it out. Sometimes it takes more than just talking to accomplish a real healthy release. Often doing something physical can help. I work with a grief support center for children in my city. In the center they have an "Emotion Commotion" room. The room is soundproofed and padded. It is equipped with a punching bag, several Nerf bats and soft instruments, and things that can be thrown. When the children need to do so, they go there to scream, hit, throw things, and cry it out. That is a healthy release. I think a stuffed pillow case hanging in the garage as a punching bag could be a great substitute for that room. Physical exertion can be a great help.

The problem is that anger does not float well. It needs to focus on something or somebody. It is not enough to be angry, we need to be angry at someone. Where your anger focuses is important. There are some places where anger seems to focus that sound wrong or even bad, but they aren't.

Sometimes anger focuses irrationally. It is not unusual for a widow to get angry at her husband for dying. He may not have had anything to do with his death, but you would be amazed at how often the widow says, "How could you leave me like this?" Then she knows she is going crazy, but, truly, that is not a bad place for the anger to focus.

Some people get mad at God. That, too, is not an unhealthy place. God is big enough to handle our anger. He knows how it feels to lose a son. If you are allowed to feel this anger and express the feelings without being confronted, this will pass and you will make peace with God anew.

Some people get mad at their physician. Why did he or she not know enough, soon enough, so your loved one would not have to die?

Many get mad at their clergy person or church.

Anger focusing on any of these areas sounds troublesome and un-healthy, but none of them are bad places for anger. *The one unhealthy place for your anger to focus is you.* Far too often, we turn the anger inside and put the blame on ourselves. It is a natural response to try to fix the blame. If we are not careful, we will become the one to blame. It may be totally irrational, but we will lay guilt on ourselves if we can figure out some connection. On a television show about Jackie Kennedy, one of her close friends told how Jackie would say that if she had just moved a little to the left, her husband would not have died. When anger focuses inward we obsessively play the game of "If Only." This game is played to some degree by everyone who is in grief, but when anger internalizes we begin to obsess on the "if only."

A lot of the guilt we feel during grief is really not guilt, it is anger turned inward. If you are playing this game over and over in your mind, it will help if you realize that anger is the real cause of that response. It helps to recognize the presence of anger. I listened to a couple tell horror tales about the failure of their minister and church after their daughter died of suicide. After an hour or so I asked them if I could tell them what I had been hearing them say. I love the phrase, "May I tell you what I heard you say?" It is so nonthreatening and lets people know you are listening. They said I could tell them. I said, "What I am hearing is that you are angry, and you should be angry." Suddenly they changed. They began talking about their anger instead of where the anger had focused. They began to say they were angry and that they had the right to be angry. In about thirty minutes time their anger shifted from an inward focus. Finally the wife said, "I have been angry at those people to keep from being angry with my daughter." The first step is to acknowledge that you are angry.

The second step may be to write out with whom you are angry. What or who do you hold responsible for your loss. How do you feel about that person? What would you like to say to them if you could? Dealing with anger on paper is not as satisfying as face to face, but it is a start. That is keeping your cussing current.

Grief is a process of dealing with whatever feelings
surface as they surface.

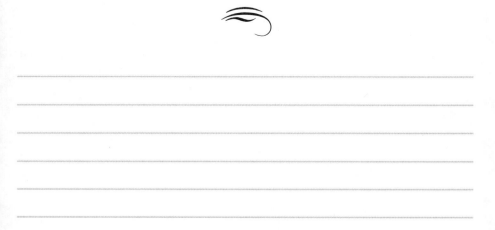

*I know of no more disagreeable
situation than to be left feeling
generally angry without anybody in
particular to be angry at.*
—Frank Moore Colby

Will it Ever Get Better?

It may seem impossible now but there will come a time when you begin to reconstruct your life. Right now that seems so far in the distant future that you can not even imagine such a thing. In the middle of such pain, it is hard to relate to a day when pain will not dominate your life. That day will come.

You will not get well. It will not be an "Okay, that is done and now I don't have to hurt anymore" sort of a deal. The best I can promise you is that one day the pain you feel will be a dull ache, but the ache will always be there. It may not be constantly on your mind. It may not even be there every day. But there will be those times when it will surface for another time of pain and memory. Something will remind you of your loved one. An anniversary or a holiday season, or something as insignificant as a flower or a butterfly will stir the feelings to a brief but intense boil. Any new loss will bring the pain to the surface for a longer stay and you will walk the valley again. Not as deep, not as dark, not as long, but very real just the same.

You will know when you turn the corner. It may be a dramatic event, or it may just be suddenly noticing that you are not in the same place with your grief, but you will know you have turned the corner in the way you cope.

One woman said, "I was walking to my car after church one Sunday and it suddenly hit me that I had to decide right then whether to live or die. I decided to live."

Or it may be there is something you cannot face now, and suddenly you can do so. A chair you cannot sit in. A closet you cannot clean. A room you cannot touch.

Another woman cleaned out the roll top desk that held all of the family pictures. She had locked it when her husband died and could not look inside. She had said the day she could open that desk would be the day she knew she was ready to live again. She called me one night and asked that I come to her home. She was standing in front of an open and clean roll top desk. She had decided to live.

You may get close to the decision many times before you actually take the step. There is no timetable. There is no hurry. A minister at one of my conferences said, "I planned to attend this conference and then go see the wife of my best friend. He died a few months ago and she still has his golf clubs in her car. I was going to tell her it was time to get those clubs out of her car. After hearing you, I think I will let her keep those clubs until she is ready to move them." He started walking away and then turned and said, "By the way, what business is it of mine if she never takes those golf clubs out of her car?"

There is no timetable for dealing with clothes, rooms, closets, personal things, or even homes and farms. Part of the process is tied up in dealing with these things when you are ready and want to do so. I often describe grief as like peeling an onion, it comes off one layer at a time and you cry a lot. If that is a good analogy, then disposing of clothing and personal items is part of that peeling.

A woman said,

> "You have just explained my husband's Packard car. He had a '55 Packard that was his pride and joy. When he died, the family insisted that I get rid of that car. I had to fight to keep it, but I won the fight. I can't tell you how much anger I worked off polishing that car. It had more chrome on it than you can imagine. I would polish a little and cuss John for dying. One morning I wanted to sell that car. I ran an ad and the first person who came bought the car. As he drove away he had the same silly looking grin on his face that my husband had the day he bought it and it was all right."

She had decided to live again.

You don't heal from the loss of a loved
one because time passes;
you heal because of what you do
with the time.

–Carol Crandall

Section III

Expectations

I Know an Angel

Who was
  Conceived in my Love
  Born in my Body
  Loved in my Being
  Gone far too Soon

And who is
  Missed in my Broken Heart
  Remembered in my Tears
  Alive in my Memories
  Living with my Heavenly Father
    on Loan until I Arrive.

Christianity is Addition
Not Subtraction

I have reached the conclusion that Christianity is addition not subtraction. God does not come in and take away the person we are, He just adds Himself to whoever we are. He does not take away the pain in our life, He just walks with us through whatever pain we must face. He does not take away who we are and how we react or how we face problems, He is just there with us. He accepts us as we are and starts walking along in our journeys no matter what they are.

That means we will walk through grief. As Christians we have the addition of His presence and ministry, but we still experience the natural responses of a grieving person. I think He does this because we grow as we walk. Christianity does not flourish well in incubators. Christianity does not have much to offer to spectators. It is when we go out into the world and experience the bad as well as the good that we grow. He does not send us broken hearts to break us or teach us, but living through the broken hearts of life tender and toughen us at the same time.

This means there are some things you can expect to face in your grief journey. I cannot list them all, but I can list some of the ones I have found to be the most prevalent. Maybe this would be a good time for you to stop and think through what I have just said. Is that the way you see it? If so, what does that mean in your understanding of how God works in our lives? There are applications to be made and thoughts to be thought. When you finish you might disagree with me totally. That, too, is healthy. I have often told the congregations I served that if I haven't said something they disagree with in the last few weeks, one of us isn't thinking. May I ask you to stop, then, and think through how God works in your life?

We do not write in order to be understood;
we write in order to understand.

–C Day-Lewis

Lonely In a Crowd

In one of my books I call grief "lonely to the bone." One of the real struggles we experience is needing someone to know how we feel and no one can do so. You are trying to describe feelings and the only tools you have to work with are words. Words just can't do that. How do you describe falling in love, for example? You can stumble around with all kinds of analogies but none really fit. Finally in desperation you say something like "when you are in love you will know it."

The same thing is true with grief. There are no words to describe how you feel. You may find someone who has experienced a similar loss and they will understand more of what you feel, but they won't really know either. I have a friend whose son died of suicide. Her best friend had a son the same age who also died of suicide one day earlier. They can give support, but neither really knows how the other one feels.

That will be almost maddening. We need to be understood. One of the basic needs of our lives is to have someone understand us. We instinctively know that having someone who understands will give us great relief. The only people we feel close to are those who have at least some interest and understanding of who we are and what we are experiencing. In the normal course of our lives, we may have many friends that we enjoy being around, but the ones we know we would count on in times of trouble are the ones who have made an effort to understand us.

We especially want our mates to understand. Most of the wear and tear of a relationship comes from not being understood. When a mate does not legitimize our thoughts or give credence to our feelings, we feel diminished. That diminishing does not go away, it builds up in our hearts and drives wedges in the relationship.

Now, more than ever, in your life you want to be understood. No one will completely understand. There will be those who are willing to hold you and love you even though they do not really know the depths of your pain. They can help. They won't take all of the lonely away, but they can at least knock the edges off of some of it.

It helps to know that these feelings are normal. You are not the only one whose friends do not understand. You are not the only one with an insensitive mate. You are not exaggerating your condition and whining over nothing. You are not unappreciative of the efforts being made by your friends. You have feelings that cannot be explained nor completely understood. That is normal and it is all right.

*We were surprised and
disappointed that people we thought were
good friends became distant, uneasy
and seemed unable to help us.
Others who were casual acquaintances
became suddenly close, sustainers of life
for us.*
–Martha Whitmore Hickman
Healing After Loss

Fear Even in Faith

I have been amazed at how fearful we become while in grief.

You may fear for your own sanity and be afraid you will not be able to make it though this ordeal. One of the most often asked questions is, "Can I survive this pain?" This is a very real concern. It is not a sign of a weak faith or a weak person. You are in more pain than you ever imagined possible. What could be more normal than worry over your capabilities to stand and fight till the end?

You may develop a great fear of what other people think or say. The first grief group I ever led totally amazed me. One of the underlying and unasked questions that hung in the room each night was, "How am I suppose to act now? If I go out to dinner with a friend, will people think I did not love enough? If I start dating, will people think it is too early and talk about me? If I break down in public, will they think I am silly and weak, or that I am just wallowing in my grief?"

One lady summed it up best when she said, "I really needed a new car, but I would not buy one for over a year. I could just hear them saying that my husband was not even cold and I was out spending his money."

I cannot make the fears go away. Facing our fears is always more helpful than just feeling them in silence. Maybe if you wrote them all out and looked at them in black and white, some of them might become less serious. Some might even become comical.

*Loneliness is to endure the presence of
one who does not understand.*

−Elbert Hubbard

Something Happened to
My Want To's

There is a form of depression that does not exemplify itself with blue feelings. This depression results in no feelings at all. You feel emotionally dead. There is a sense of being detached from reality. You feel as if you are standing off to one side watching yourself perform but not really involved or feeling much. This type of depression is very prevalent in grieving. Your mind and emotions will protect themselves even if they have to shut down. In the intensity of grieving, the emotions often just stop working.

You may experience "brown out." Your mind will not function. You may get lost in your regular grocery store. You may forget things until you begin to think you have developed Alzheimer's disease. If you do not recognize this as normal you may find yourself in almost a state of panic. These "brown outs" are your mind taking care of itself. They will pass.

The lack of emotions can have an effect on your marriage. This can be especially true in the sexual part of the relationship. The male may not notice any difference in his interest or enjoyment of sex. Sex to the female is much more of an emotional experience than it is for the male. Since the female is likely to be emotionally dead, her sexual interest is often greatly diminished. One woman whose son died said, "I just feel gutted inside. I have no emotions to give." If the male does not develop a great deal of understanding and patience, this can become a struggle added to the burden. If he can accept this as a normal reaction that will pass in time, then the struggle can lessen. The woman can also help by being sensitive to his needs even though it will not be the same for her until the emotions restore themselves.

The major hope for this book is to make you understand that you are normal. Nothing that I know of helps people in their grief like the discovery that they are normal. That it is all right to feel what they feel. That it is all right not to feel what they don't feel.

I try to help people avoid what I call "The feel bad because you feel bad syndrome." This syndrome happens when you have a feeling and tell yourself, "I should not feel that way." Then you say, "there is something wrong with me or I wouldn't feel that way." This leads to, "therefore there is something wrong with me." That syndrome snowballs until you become a basket case of fears and phobias.

Feel what you feel and don't worry about the rest.

*One doesn't discover new lands
without consenting to lose sight of the
shore for a very long time.*

–André Gide

Section IV

Gifts for the Journey

*I am a more sensitive person, a more effective
pastor, a more sympathetic counselor because of my
son Aaron's life and death than I would ever have been
without it. And I would give up all those
gains in a second if I could
have my son back. I would forgo all spiritual growth
and depth which has come my way because of our
experience and be what I was fifteen
years ago—an average rabbi, an indifferent
counselor, helping some people and unable to help
others and the father of a bright, happy boy.
But, I cannot choose.*

–Rabbi Harold Kushner
*When Bad Things Happen
to Good People*

The Gift of a Message

Because God loved us, He gave us freedom and started us on a journey called life. Then He bankrupted Heaven being sure we never had to walk alone. He does not intrude on our freedoms. He does not force cures upon us. He does not take away all struggle and pain, but He does provide for us. Christians do not have some ticket that allows them to avoid grief, but they do have resources from God that give unique help and comfort in the pain.

We have a God we can discover and lean on. We have His own words of comfort to read in the darkest of times. We have a faith that somehow lets us know we are not alone. We have an open invitation to talk to him directly. We have His followers who walk with us. He did not set it up so His children would not suffer, but He made sure they did not do so alone.

A woman whose husband and daughter were both killed by drunk drivers six years apart told me of her losses and then said something that I found to be shocking. She said, "When my husband died, your books were the only ones I would read. My husband was a minister so I received a lot of books, but the Scriptures in the books made me angry." That woman and her family are wonderful and dedicated Christians. They attend an evangelical church and are deep into studying the Bible. Yet she said the same Bible she still loves made her angry after her husband died.

I have had many visits with this family and we have discussed the reasons for this many times. People in grief are very sensitive to being trivialized. We don't want our grief explained away. We do not want someone to diminish the impact or the importance of what has happened to us. We get very defensive about the size and depth of our hurt. If we reduce the importance of our grief we also reduce the importance of our loved one's life and death. There certainly is nothing wrong with the Bible. The problem is that the texts quoted most often, and the texts people are most comfortable with if they have not experienced grief, are the ones that trivialize the death.

Twenty years from now I can tell you that all things work together for those who love the Lord, and you will feel blessed by those words. The morning after your loved one died, those same words seem to say that your pain is a minor thing in the overall scheme of things and that one day it will not matter at all. That morning you needed to hear that someone understands you have been hurt to the bone and will never get over it.

People will tell you that "God will not put more on you than you can bear," and expect that to make you feel less of a burden. Instead of feeling better, you feel trivialized. You may want to scream, "Are you saying this is not a very large burden? Are you saying this is just a minor thing?" I do not want to argue theology in this book, but I think what the Scripture really says is that we will not meet any temptation we cannot escape. I sort of feel like I face more than I can carry on a very regular basis. If that were not so, I would not need to spend near as much time in prayer for strength and guidance.

This does not mean you will not find comfort in the Scriptures. They may well become the most comforting words of all to you, but you will need the freedom to select the ones that have meaning for you. I find it amazing how certain scriptures will come to mind and give me comfort and insight. Often these are scriptures I have not thought of in a very long time. Often I find meaning there that I cannot explain to anyone else. It means something to me that it does not mean to anyone else. Recently a father, whose daughter was killed in a church van on the way to summer camp, quoted a text to me and proceeded to tell me what he found in those words. I could not see any way to find the same meaning in those words, but they spoke to him. I concluded that the spirit of God speaks and interprets words of comfort to the individual ear of His children.

That means you alone will have to be the judge of how much the scriptures help you in this time of pain, and you alone will have to be the one to choose which scriptures do the blessing. I hope you find some words that allow you, in your weariness and with a heavy laden heart, to come close and find rest.

Treat the other man's faith gently;
it is all he has to believe with.
–Henry S. Haskins

The Gift of an Ear

One of the great shocks of my life happened when I started studying and speaking about grief. As a minister, I assumed that prayer would automatically be the resource for anyone in grief. I fully expected to hear story after story about how prayer sustained and comforted when nothing else could help. I expected people to tell me that prayer made the pain go away and they were miraculously healed of their grief.

Instead of what I expected I began to hear wonderful Christians say that they found it hard to pray. Not that they did not believe in prayer, but they found it hard to actually pray, and often felt their prayers stopped at the ceiling in the room. They could not feel connected to God. When I got over my shock, I began trying to understand what was going on. Prayer is very special to me and I want it to help those in grief.

A great deal of the problem comes from your not being able to concentrate on prayer. In grief you will not be able to concentrate on anything for very long. This book is written in short bursts because of that very thing. If someone handed you a thick book with small print, you could not bear to even open the first page. It would be overwhelming to you. In grief, prayer must also be done in short bursts. A quick glance toward God is about as long as you will be able to concentrate. Luckily the Scriptures tell us that He interprets even our groaning. He doesn't require well-worded prayers.

As we talked about in an earlier chapter, your grief leaves you emotionally exhausted. We are accustomed to prayer being an emotion. We feel close to God when we pray. We sense that He is listening. When the emotional deadness comes we can't feel these same emotions when we pray. It is easy to think God is not listening or that we are not getting through. This does not happen to everyone, of course. I have heard other people tell of having even more of a sense of closeness in prayer during their grief. I am telling you about it in case you are having a struggle with prayer and feel deserted by God. What you feel is not unusual. What you feel is not from a lack of faith or a lack of prayer's power. Pray when you can in any way you can and trust the Father to hear even if it does not feel as though He is. In time, the feelings will return.

One of the most remarkable things to me is that God will listen to us at all. I remember reading about an old mountaineer who listened to the national broadcast of the great orchestras that once were common on Sunday afternoons. He wrote the network that he wanted to play along with the orchestra but he had no way to tune his fiddle. The next Sunday they stopped this national broadcast and the orchestra played an "A" so one old mountaineer could tune his fiddle. That has always reminded me of a God who would stop what He was doing to lend me His ear. If that is all prayer is, it is more than enough for me. Just knowing that God will hear me is plenty.

God listens to our weeping when the occasion itself is beyond our knowledge, but still within His love and power.

–Daniel A. Poling

The Gift of Community

It sounds holy to say, "All I need is Jesus," and it sounds like a statement of faith to sing, "Christ Is All I Need," but those statements are neither true nor are they Biblical. The Bible is replete with the concept of Christians helping one another.

Galatians 6 tells us to "bear one anther's burdens and so fulfill the law of Christ" (NKJV).

II Corinthians 1:3 says:
> Praise be to the God and Father of our Lord Jesus Christ, the all-merciful Father, the God whose consolation never fails us! He comforts us in all our troubles, so that we in turn may be able to comfort others in any trouble of theirs and to share with them the consolation we ourselves receive from God. (NEB)

It does not diminish the work or power of God to say that people need people. He made us to need each other and did so on purpose. His great plan for our lives is for us to love one another. What better way to love, than giving comfort and strength to a friend?

He created us to need Him, and to need one another. Nothing takes the place of the work of God in our lives. Nothing can compare with the power of His love. Nothing can even imitate that power. It is also true that nothing takes the place of the work of God's people in our lives. We need both.

That is particularly true as you face your grief. It feels great to know that God is there and cares. It also feels great to have a warm body standing near also loving you. You will find help in your friends. There is great help available in the grief support groups that are available almost everywhere. These groups were unheard of a few years ago, but their help has been discovered and offered by many different organizations. I urge everyone to consider a group experience.

The one great gift you can receive from people is the gift of significance. I know of nothing that is more healing in grief. I also know no source for significance other than a listening ear from a human being.

When things happen to us the first thing we need to do, and the first thing we want to do, is to establish the significance of that event. We want to tell the world what has happened to us. I have watched the television coverage of many wrecks, fires, tornadoes and explosions. Almost without exception, the eye witnesses will tell how they felt and what happened to them before they even mention any victims at all. "It nearly scared me to death, I ran into the house and just had to sit down." "Something like this just doesn't happen here." "I don't think I will ever get over the shock." These are statements from eye witnesses, not the victims. It is human nature to want to tell someone. It is a basic need to establish the significance of the event.

When the event is something that happens to us and we are more than eye witnesses, the need to establish significance becomes even greater. If we cannot do so, we cannot move through the experience toward healing. If no one listens, or if they trivialize your experience, you try again and again to find some way to get the story heard and the significance understood. If none can be found, the experience and the hurt can become an obsession to you. I know many people who are still obsessing over a loss that happened sixty years ago. No one allowed them the right to significance.

Over the years I have studied long term hurts and grudges. I am convinced that a grudge does not happen because someone is too hardheaded to forgive. Grudges happen because someone is hurt and they never get to establish the significance of that hurt. Over time that hurt becomes a grudge and tends to dominate their personality.

The first step forward in your grief walk is establishing the significance of the person and the significance of *the* loss. Early in your grieving experience there will be a very natural urge to talk about the person who has died. It is almost as if you must find out for yourself how wonderful they were. No one really knows how much a person meant until they are gone. Then there is a period when we are discovering their true value in our lives. Every day you will think of some other attribute of their lives, or something else you want to tell them, or some experience you remember with joy. It is almost as if you must inventory the loss before you can grieve it. Folks will think you are wallowing in your grief and you are, and you should. Wallowing is healthy. Wallowing is needed. Wallow until you have thought through and expressed every wonderful thing about the one you have loved.

You also need to establish the significance of *your* loss. This is when trivialization makes you angry. You desperately need someone to see the depths of your pain. If someone tries to put the best face on your loss, or explain how you should be grateful that it could have been worse, or that you should not weep because your loved one is better off, you will experience a strange seething inside. You may wonder why you are reacting so strongly, but you are doing so because these explanations are shutting off your chance at the significance you need.

Establishing the social significance of your loved one's life is also necessary. When someone calls their name and tells how much they miss them, you will cry and feel warm at the same time. You will not be able to get enough of hearing people praise this life that meant so much to you.

The ear is the most healing part of the human body. God made us so we need to be heard. He could have made us so we had no need of any help from anyone other than Him, but He chose not to do so. I think He made a great choice. When you are heard, you are blessed. When you are heard, the one furnishing the ear is also blessed. Find some good ears and wear them out. They will love it as much as you will need it.

We are all here on earth to help others.
What on earth the others are here for
I don't know.

 —W. H. Auden

The Gift of Presence

When I was a very young minister, I received a frantic call one morning telling me about a mother finding her baby dead in the crib. I had never heard of Sudden Infant Death Syndrome, and had no idea what to say or do when I arrived at the home. I walked into a chaotic scene of several women physically restraining the mother to keep her away from the baby. As soon as I walked in they began telling me that I must help them. They said the mother should not touch her baby's body. I had no idea whether that was right or not. Just as I started toward the mother, someone said, "Mr. Lockstone is here." Mr. Lockstone was the funeral director. I can not describe the feeling that swept through the room the moment someone said he had arrived. Relief is too mild a term. Someone had arrived who knew what to do. I will never forget that feeling.

Mr. Lockstone waved the women out of the room, sat the mother on the couch, and handed her baby to her. He said, "Now, you sit right there and hold your baby as long as you want to. There is no hurry. When you are ready I will take care of everything." He never said another word. I watched in amazement as the power of presence did its work. She rocked her baby for a little while, and then placed his body in Mr. Lockstone's hands.

My wife had very serious bypass surgery. We were three hundred miles from our home and the surgery was an emergency. I had no idea whether or not she would survive. Sometime that afternoon, three women from our church walked into the waiting room. They did not bring a cure. They did not do anything to make things any better. But their presence gave me a lift I cannot describe. That, too, is the power of presence.

My grandson died. He was born on Christmas Eve and died Christmas Day. He only lived thirty-four hours. Just before he died, they took away all of the tubes and wires and brought him to us to love. We all held him until he died. I am a minister, his other grandfather is a minister, and his father is a minister, and as soon as he died none of us knew what to do next. We sat staring at one another and felt as helpless as children. Then the funeral director walked in. The "Mr. Lockstone" feelings returned. He would know what to do. He would take care of us. We were not alone in our loss. He brought the power of presence to our lives.

The remarkable thing about the book of Job is not that Job lost everything, nor is it that his friends added to his problem instead of bringing comfort. The remarkable thing to me is that God did not answer any of Job's questions, *not one*. He just overwhelmed Job with His presence. That does not sound like much, but somehow Job went from saying he wished he had never been born, or, if he had to be, he wished he had died as soon as he was born, he went from that to, "For I know that my redeemer liveth…"(Job 19:25 KJV)   That is the power of presence.

At a recent conference a young mother was wearing a large button with her daughter's picture printed on the front. I see these kinds of buttons at almost every conference. These buttons help parents establish the significance of their lost child. I made it a point to visit with this mother and she told me her daughter was born with a congenital problem. They thought they had won the battle and the daughter was going to be fine. On a school trip, the daughter suddenly relapsed and, in a few days, she died. We talked for several minutes and then the program started and I had to go speak.

This mother waited after the speech so she could tell me the rest of her story. She said, that during the time when they thought her daughter was well, she woke up in the night greatly troubled. She got up and found that her husband was still up so she asked him the question that had awakened her. She said, "How do people live through the loss of a child? How do they survive?" Her husband said that he did not know, but that he supposed their faith helped them. She said, "But I have no faith." That night haunted her thoughts for some time. Then her daughter died. She said that a few weeks after her daughter's death she was so overwhelmed with grief that her legs crumpled and she fell to the floor. She could not find the strength to get up, so she lay there in tears. She said, "Suddenly I was overwhelmed with the presence of God. I felt warm all over. I knew He was in the room. I don't know how I knew that.

Suddenly I knew I was loved. I knew I was not alone. I knew, but I had no idea how, that I would make it."

She said, "That night did not cure me. That night did not take away all of my problems or all of my questions. But, since that night, I have never again felt alone."

God is still in the presence business.

The presence of God may not come to you
in a dramatic overwhelming rush.

The crushed emotions and the mind in turmoil
may make it harder to find and feel.

God does not yell nor does He force,
His voice is small and still.

My prayer is that you will feel His presence
and know you are not alone.

Have courage for the great sorrows of
life, and patience for the small ones.
And when you have laboriously
accomplished your daily task, go to sleep
in peace. God is awake.

–Victor Hugo

The Gift of Hope

May I tell you why I believe in Heaven? The easy answer would be to say the Bible tells me so and, of course, that has a profound effect on my believing. I am sure my being raised in a church also gives great credence to my belief. I must confess, however, that I was afraid of Heaven when I was a child. It seemed far too long. The fact that there was never an end to eternity was more than I could ever comprehend. Heaven seemed far too boring to a busy young boy, and way too much church stuff for my liking. Who wants to sit around on a cloud all day playing the harp? The streets may be gold, but I kept hearing the preachers talk about singing and praying all night and getting to hear Paul preach, and a ten year old mind just can't see that as very heavenly.

I remember hearing an old professor from Mississippi say something about how God had eight octillion suns in His universe and then he said, "Don't miss being there when the big show starts." Somehow Heaven changed. I began seeing it as freedom to explore the universe unencumbered by time or space. We will know the height and depth of all God has made. Wow!

And we shall have all knowledge. Where now we see through a glass darkly, as Paul said, then we shall know even as also we are known. The question about Heaven I am most often asked is, "Will we know each other there?" I always answer with, "Do you think we are going to be dumber there than we are here?"

But with all of that said, I must confess that I believe in Heaven because I must do so. The Apostle Paul said that having hope only in this life leaves us miserable. He was right.

Let me tell you about a young woman named Katie. She was talented, brilliant, lovely and loving. She was a ballerina who thrilled audiences with her beauty and charm. She had a loving family that was extremely close and supportive. Her life had not been without struggle. Her father was killed in a plane crash when she was nine years of age. There was not much available in those days to help her walk the grief journey. This left her with scars she had to fight and pain she had to live with, but she did fight and she did live.

Katie was brutally murdered. Cold, unfeeling, senselessly murdered. My life has been one of being involved with many such tragedies. It has been my lot to try to help families survive these horrors that seem to be happening with greater and greater frequency. If there is no life beyond life, then I have stood by too many graves and tried to comfort too many mothers.

If this is all there is then:
Evil wins;
All hope is gone;
Nothing makes sense.

If there is life beyond life, then I can live even through man's inhumanity to man. The realization that this is not the whole story, that there will be a time when we understand, and that there is life beyond life is absolutely necessary for me to continue.

I can stand next to the tragedies and sadness mainly because of these few words:

...I will come again
and receive you to Myself;
that where I am, there you will be also.
—Jesus of Nazareth
John 14:3 NKJV

Parable of the Twins

Once upon a time, twin boys were conceived in the same womb. Weeks passed, and the twins developed. As their awareness grew, they laughed for joy: "Isn't it great that we were conceived? Isn't it great to be alive?"

Together the twins explored their world. When they found their mother's cord that gave them life, they sang for joy: "How great is our mother's love that she shares her own life with us!"

As weeks stretched into months the twins noticed how much each was changing. "What does it mean?" asked the one. "It means that our stay in this world is drawing to an end," said the other one. "But I don't want to go," said the other one. "I want to stay here always." "We have no choice," said the other. "But maybe there is life after birth!" "But how can there be?" responded the one. "We will shed our life cord, and how is life possible without it? Besides, we have seen evidence that others were here before us, and none of them have returned to tell us that there is life after birth. No, this is the end."

And so the one fell into deep despair, saying: "If conception ends in birth, what is the purpose of life in the womb? It's meaningless! Maybe there is no mother after all." "But there has to be," protested the other. "How else did we get here? How do we remain alive?"

"Have you ever seen our mother?" said the one. "Maybe she lives only in our minds. Maybe we made her up because the idea made us feel good."

And so the last days in the womb were filled with deep questioning and fear. Finally, the moment of birth arrived.

When the twins had passed from their world, they opened their eyes and they cried. For what they saw exceeded their fondest dreams.

Eye has not seen, nor ear heard,
Nor have entered into the heart of man
The things which God has prepared for those who love Him
1 Corinthians 2:9 (NKJV)

*Faith is the little night-light that burns in
a sick room; as long as it is there, the
obscurity is not complete, we turn towards
it and await the daylight.*

—Abbé Henri Huvelin

Bibliography

The Scripture quotations in this book are from three translations.

Those marked KJV are from the *King James Version.*

Those marked NEB are from *The New English Bible.* Cambridge: The University Printing House, 1961, 1970.

Those marked NKJV are from the *New King James Version.* Nashville: Thomas Nelson, Inc., 1982.

The quotes in this book have been gathered from many collections. The authors/editors of these books have spent a great deal of time selecting meaningful and poignant messages which speak to the grieving soul and we are grateful for their efforts.

Hickman, Martha Whitmore. *Healing After Loss: Daily Meditations for Working Through Grief.* New York: Avon Books, 1994. ISBN 0-380-77338-4

McNess, Pat, ed. *Dying: A Book of Comfort.* Garden City, New York: Doubleday Direct, Inc. 1996 ISBN 0-446-67400-1

Staudacher, Carol. *A Time to Grieve: Meditations for Healing After the Death of a Loved One.* San Francisco: HarperCollins, 1994. ISBN 0-06-250845-8

Zadra, Dan and Marcia Woodard, comp. *Forever Remembered: A Gift for the Grieving Heart.* Seattle, Washington: Compendium, Inc., 1997. ISBN 1-888387-20-3

Selected Resources from In-Sight Books

by Doug Manning

Grief
Don't Take My Grief Away From Me
The Gift of Significance
The Special Care Series
Lean On Me Gently–Helping the Grieving Child
Thoughts for the Lonely Nights journal and CD

Elder Care
Aging is a Family Affair
Parenting Our Parents
Searching for Normal Feelings
Share My Lonesome Valley–The Slow Grief of Long-Term Care
Socks–How to Solve Problems
Visiting in a Nursing Home
When Love Gets Tough–Making the Nursing Home Decision

Other Resources from In-Sight Books
I Know Someone Who Died coloring book by Connie Manning
The Empty Chair–The Journey of Grief After
Suicide by Beryl Glover
The Shattered Dimension–The Journey of Grief After
Suicide video by Beryl Glover
What to Do When the Police Leave by Bill Jenkins
Comfort Cards bereavement card collection
Framed Art including the Parable of the Twins

For a complete catalog or ordering
information contact:
In-Sight Books, Inc.
1-800-658-9262
www.insightbooks.com
books@ionet.net

Doug Manning

His career has included minister, counselor, business executive, author and publisher. He and his wife, Barbara, have been parents to four daughters and long-term caregivers to three parents.

After thirty years in the ministry, Doug began a new career in 1982. He now devotes his time to writing, counseling and leading seminars in the areas of grief and elder care. His publishing company, In-Sight Books, Inc., specializes in books, video and audio tapes specifically designed to help people face some of the toughest challenges of life.

Doug has a warm, conversational style in which he shares insights from his various experiences. Sitting down to read a book from Doug is like having a long conversation with a good friend.